A SLOW DANCE IN MEMORIAM

And Other Poems

Wanda Penalver Bevan

Copyright © Wanda Penalver Bevan, 2022
Published 2022 by The Book Reality Experience

ISBN: 978-1-922670-51-9 - Paperback Edition
ISBN: 978-1-922670-52-6 - EBook Edition

All rights reserved.

The right of Wanda Penalver Bevan to be identified as author of this Work has been asserted by her in accordance with sections 77 and 78 of the Copyright, Designs and Patents Act 1988.

This book is a work of fiction and any resemblance to actual persons, living or dead, is purely coincidental.

No part of this publication may be reproduced, stored in retrieval system, copied in any form or by any means, electronic, mechanical, photocopying, recording or otherwise transmitted without written permission from the publisher. You must not circulate this book in any format.

Table of Contents

Preface i

I. Pandemic 1

    A Slow Dance In Memoriam 3

    Triumvirate 4

    Nowhere Left To Run 6

    We Mourn The Year 9

II. Love's Obsession 11

    I Have Fallen Into Your Eyes 13

    Cellular Sentiments 14

    Recess 15

    A Bucket For Your Tears 16

    Chunks Of White Peaches 17

    November Pictures 18

    Climb Inside 19

III. Love's Wounds 21

    Permanent Scar 23

    Home Decorating 24

    A Waxing Gibbous 25

    Before Gpses 26

    Swim Lesson 27

    Broken 28

IV. Love's Revelations 29

- April's Breath 31
- Whispers On A Winter's Day Far Away 32
- Stay Close By 33
- Ballet 34
- Seasons 35
- Love Somewhat Later 37
- While You Slept 38

V. Loneliness 39

- A Box Under The Stairs 41
- Where I Crouch Not Moving 42
- Triple Digits 43
- Layovers And Divorces 45
- Haven't Met You 47
- Hiding 48

VI. Introspection 49

- Little Drummer Girl 51
- August 25th 52
- The Taste Of Coffee 53
- An Ode To Writer's Block 56
- Discoveries At The Park 58
- Of This I Am Certain 59

VII. America 61
    America's Child 63
    For Trayvon 65
    Ballot 66
About The Author 67
Acknowledgements 69

For all those who feel things deeply

PREFACE

Dividing this collection into sections was more difficult than I expected. I think most creative writers will agree that any kind of non-creative task we do with our writing ends up birthing some kind of creative element. This process—attempting to divide these poems into groups—was nearly as challenging as writing the poems themselves.

    I didn't do much writing during the pandemic. In fact, I did almost no writing during the pandemic. The motivation to use the time in isolation to write that next great novel, short story, stage play, song, screenplay, or to paint, sketch, sculpt, dance, film, video, whatever artistic thing that artists are expected to create, didn't happen to me. The guilt was debilitating until I talked to other artists and learned many of them weren't artistically motivated during 2020 either. The truth is, there are times we artists, like everyone else, need to just be quiet. Not "quiet" as in we don't want to talk to anyone, although that's completely legitimate as well, but "quiet" as in, there's a place we sometimes go—need to go—where it's okay to embrace the parts of ourselves that possess an inability to create. It's a place where we want to feel human and not artistic. And when we go there, we feel guilty. We crave free time to devote to our craft, and when the abundance of free time resulting from the Covid-19 shut down fell into our laps, it only made sense that our creativity should simply flow. Not the case. Because, like everyone else, we too experienced the physical and psychological impact of the pandemic, and each of us differently. I'm not sure why publishing these poems now feels like the appropriate time. Perhaps the isolation of the pandemic solidified my poetic voice enough to finally share them with you.

After much wrangling, I did break the poems into the following sections.

PANDEMIC. If going through 2020 helped me clarify my poetic voice, it seemed fitting to make this the first section. As I explained above, I did little to no writing during Covid, so there are only four poems in this part. I struggled with whether to open with *A Slow Dance in Memoriam*, the title of the collection, and instead start with *Nowhere Left to Run*, which summarizes my experience during the shutdown. But *A Slow Dance in Memoriam* reveals the main character traits that define me and therefore, show up in all my writing: my love for music, my ability to feel things deeply, my thoughts on current events, and my tireless fascination with the power of love. So it seemed the appropriate poem to introduce myself to you.

LOVE'S OBSESSION, LOVE'S WOUNDS, and *LOVE'S REVELATIONS* are about the men I've loved who knowingly or unknowingly inspired me to write. Whether the sentiment is joyful or painful, the writings in *LOVE'S OBSESSION* share a sense of naiveté we all experience when we fall in love, especially when we're young. That doesn't mean we don't experience obsession in love as we age. We can and do. I was torn between *LOVE'S OBSESSION* and "Love's Blindness" for the title of this section and decided "obsession" more fully summarized the euphoria, fantasy, and delusion found in some of these poems. *LOVE'S WOUNDS* are writings inspired by the hurt we experience in love, and, for what it's worth, I believe the age-old theory that if we're going to love at all, we will get hurt. *LOVE'S REVELATIONS* speaks to just that—seeing things clearly in love. Regardless of what we discover, the place we look from, and the individual we look upon, comes with greater understanding than when we're obsessed.

The poems in *INTROSPECTION* touch on my relationship with self, family, life, in general. *August 25th*, the date my mother died, was that defining moment when we realize that even though we may be fully grown, the severance of the umbilical cord is never so profound as when we lose a parent. *Discoveries in the Park*, inspired by my first child, came to me with the same impact—the realization that the parent-child relationship is the only human relationship intended to grow towards separation. These two poems reveal an attempt to confront the joy and grief entwined in those relationships. You may find *Of This I'm Certain* to be more about romance than introspection, and therefore out of place in this section. I confess, when I wrote it, it was about romance. But over time, it seemed to hold a deeper meaning about life itself, the knowledge that life is short, that our days here are limited, that it's okay to go dancing, in fact—imperative—that we go dancing, because "it will be midnight soon", and we will have to say goodnight. Forever.

LONELINESS. It was simply loneliness that was the driving force behind this group of poems. *Triple Digits* chronicles one afternoon a few months after my divorce. Typically, I'd attribute the empty street at lunch hour to the miserable temperatures, but all I could feel was the desolation as it related to my own circumstances. The last line, 'if my only companion would be no more than a song' was a stepping back from what I hoped was *aloneness*, to acknowledge that it was *loneliness*. *Where I Crouch Not Moving* is an attempt to capture the sight and sound of loneliness. Although each of us experiences loneliness differently, the metaphor for me was a wild animal that wounds you before killing you. And because I have a terrifying phobia of rodents, the image is imminent death by rats.

AMERICA. I will never accept the violence inflicted by human beings against each other based on our differences, whether it be race, nationality, religion, political beliefs, or gender identity. (I understand this list is incomplete, and I apologize to readers belonging to a marginalized group that I unintentionally failed to include here). Note, the first sentence of this paragraph is not "I will never understand the violence…" I *do* understand it. But I will never *accept* it. *America's Child* was written in 1995 when the Federal Building in Oklahoma City was bombed, resulting in the death of 168 people, many of them children. My oldest daughter was three years old at the time, the same age as most of the children who perished in the building's daycare facility that morning. I won't glorify the name of the perpetrator here (just as I won't glorify the name of the gunman who shot Trayvon Martin while he innocently walked through a neighborhood in Sanford, Florida), but when it was revealed he was American, it struck me that we, as a country, were collectively responsible for raising this person from childhood to grow up and walk among us. That feeling turned into a question I heard over and over in my head, which became the first line of the poem: *"O, Beautiful for Spacious Skies, how have we let our children die?"* The references to other anthems seemed to follow naturally from there. As I write this, almost three decades since Oklahoma, this type of violence has only worsened with time. I wrote *Ballot* the day after the 2016 presidential election. I believe that's the only reference necessary.

I read somewhere that the purpose of a novel is to make the reader feel what the characters are feeling, and the purpose of a poem is to make the reader feel what the writer is feeling. Thank you for allowing me to share my feelings with you.

WPB

I.
PANDEMIC

A SLOW DANCE IN MEMORIAM

The newsfeed said he died at 81
and cocooned in my sadness
I sat motionless and followed my mind
to where it goes when I'm sad
But you took my hand and led me to
the center of the floor and
we slow danced while he serenaded
us from YouTube
Swaying to the music as the lovely day
turned to dusk, just the two of us in a
room growing dimmer with no sunshine,
quarantined in a world that makes
no sense to me but knowing the woman
I'll be when it's over has been changed
by your love

TRIUMVIRATE

At this moment of what I'm certain are only
the tree and the sky
though I could speak of other things in view
from this window
the grass below on the greenbelt, the birds that
decorate the silence
with their delicious relentlessness
like the fowls in Matthew 6:26 that *sow not, neither do they reap*
never worrying where their next meal is coming from
    yet here I sit
unsure whether the things I need will be on
the grocery store shelf today
they weren't there yesterday

    and I sit
studying the tree that reminds me life is steadfast yet
ever changing
the same tree transformed from season to season
yet remains perpetually itself
the same sky whose clouds were giant cotton balls when
I was a little girl
then became real clouds when I became a woman

> *I sit*

knowing all that's happening in the world with no way
to change it
surrendering to my powerlessness
desperate in my insignificance
longing to be worthy of this new triumvirate

the tree
the sky
and me

NOWHERE LEFT TO RUN

It's been easy running from it
excuses lined up like empty cans on a
backyard fence—*I've only seen people do
that in movies, shoot empty cans lined up on
a backyard fence*

—if I'd ever seen that in real life or
ever held a gun maybe I could shoot
my excuses
daily death toll numbers and
percentage of positive cases
who would have thought along with
triple digit temps
and grand views of the Grand
Canyon, Arizona would
one day be famous for highest Covid
numbers
it's okay because I can run from it

joining the work from home tribe,
deciding which
destination—*post office or drugstore or gas
station or supermarket*—will win most

adventurous choice of the day—*living
room to kitchen to bedroom to kitchen to
living room to bedroom*—gas station
usually loses because there isn't much
need for gas these days
most days there is no destination

imagining if my parents were still
alive and what it would
be like if they were sick and I could
only wave at them
through a nursing home window
hoping they were strong enough to
wave back or at least smile—*or if they
couldn't see me at all*—the
thought nauseates me so I run from it

conversations with my children and
after each one ends I
wonder when I'll see them in person
again
then try to imagine if I never saw
them again—*but I can't imagine that, so I
don't*—and the pain makes it the
easiest thought of all
to run from

walks with my lover in the spring,
before spring became a pandemic
but we can't take long walks now
because it's too hot outside
so instead we reminisce about the

first time we did—*when we saw in each
other's eyes that we belonged together*—I
imagine my life without him and have
to run

the only place left to run is
to my creative demon
stalking me from every corner of my
isolation
while I listen to it moan and sob
and sob and moan in the middle of
the night
abandoned and confused just like I
am
by this hell
and though I cannot save it, cannot
stop its suffering
it's the only place to go now
where I still recognize the world
with nothing left it is all that is left
with no peace of mind it is peace of
mind
with no vaccine it is vaccine

so I return

WE MOURN THE YEAR

We mourn the year
We mourn its death and its cruel
bequests
of loss of life, of broken spirit,
of painful isolation, of debilitating
doubt,
of fractured faith, of paralyzing fear,
of unbridled hatred, of absence of
understanding
We stare at the calendar and
anticipate the day when light
penetrates darkness
And with the light, we seek the hope
we thought betrayed us
We mourn, though it may be with
anger
We mourn, as we concede our frailty
We mourn, because we must
And with the hope that lies beneath
the rubble of all that we've endured,
because we must, WE RISE

II.

LOVE'S OBSESSION

I HAVE FALLEN INTO YOUR EYES

A crescendo of orchestras roared
to my spinning
I looked up and saw
>   *cerulean*

down and saw
>   *jade*

then laser beams of
>   *amber*

turned into
>   *pewter*

ribbons that tossed my weightless body
at rocket speed through ten thousand years of light
please don't stop this joy ride of my soul
>   *I*
>   *have*
>   *fallen*
>   *into*
>   *your*
>   *eyes*

and never before this moment knew I could fly

CELLULAR SENTIMENTS

Stuck somewhere between writer's block
and not being able to talk to you
I found myself running scared
but scared implies *a state of fear*
and it's not fear I have for the way the
road ahead may bend, as roads—at some point—
eventually will
So while I wait for *in a few days* to become
in a few minutes
I will run unafraid towards
the wonderland of our next conversation
I'll pause to swim naked in a bottomless pond
of irresistibly invented notions
then wrap myself up in the
memory of your voice to keep warm

RECESS

Come play with me in a playground where
words are uninvited guests
and you and I are the hosts to all our needs
where sundown and sunrise take
second place to our breathing
and our souls are blackout curtains
to the world outside
where the only thing my heart recognizes
is the sound of the beating of yours
where anything other than you
is nothing I have a need for
and all roads leading back to where you were
before you found me
erode more with each of your kisses

A BUCKET FOR YOUR TEARS

Here, use my bucket
for your tears
and whether it holds a single drop
or overflows past the brim
I'll carry it some place far away
and come back to you
with it empty

Whether it takes
three journeys or three hundred
I'll come back

CHUNKS OF WHITE PEACHES

They brought it over in a Tupperware container,
fresh peaches and a handful of blueberries
soaked all day in vodka and peach schnapps
with a hint of cilantro
So delicious everyone commented
including me
Sipping it all day
my only clear thought by nightfall was

you and me

together hand in hand jumping into it
chunks of white peaches the size of our heads
floating around us
kicking blueberries out of the way
as we swam
seeing who could make the
best bubbles underwater by
mouthing the words
I love you

NOVEMBER PICTURES

The dogs posed on top of the rock as if for a portrait
the kind that makes me wish I were a painter
As always their faces were not expressionless and
when our eyes met I looked for sadness that I was
driving away
I laughed at my ego then
reached the curve I told you about last night
the peak was different but no less beautiful
What was black against a silver sky had donned
its foliaceous coat to greet the morning
I steered slowly around the curve
partly for safety
partly to take with me as much
of the scene as I could
before reaching town
It's cold outside your arms, have I told you?
I have so much to tell you, can we take our time?
I will not say the quiet of your canyon can
ease the pain of leaving your bed
only your eyes looking into mine will do

CLIMB INSIDE

Climb inside my skin
Because any farther away
from me is too far

III.

LOVE'S WOUNDS

PERMANENT SCAR

I don't know where I was when I felt you lingering
On the heels of a song I guess
or upon waking I found you there like before
    when I knew who I was
Last night the moderator said
"if soulmates are real does that mean
they have an obligation to the universe to meet?"
    I knew the answer
but the question I had
was *what does it mean if they*
don't—meet?
    I didn't ask it out loud
There is no unpairing of hearts entwined
no escape when souls merge together
There is only running
and running
and running
from the part of yourself you no longer recognize

HOME DECORATING

You may have noticed I painted
all the doors in colors you like
because I know
that near them is where you'll feel most
at ease

A WAXING GIBBOUS

He was the one who taught her
all the phases of the moon
and when he said goodbye, her tears
became a storm on the horizon
He said *don't cry* and told her life
was still worth living
but she didn't feel alive
He showed her people were
laughing but she felt she'd
never laugh again
He lifted her chin to see the love
that surrounded her
but still, she felt unloved
For he was the one who taught her
all the phases of the moon
and with him gone, the moon
would never again be what it was
the moon that hangs low enough to touch
the moon that controls the tide
the moon whose light she hoped might
someday guide him back to her

BEFORE GPSes

another dead end/another wrong turn on
the highway
too dark to read the map/too late to care
guess we should have
pulled over sooner/paid more attention
passing the exit that was ours/shouting too loudly
to realize any one of them would do

SWIM LESSON

Immersed in this sparkling pool now
up to our chins
the water nurtures us like a loving mother
That I am not a swimmer may be the only thing
about me you don't know
and while you most likely are perfectly skilled
at treading water
if we should discover that
all this time the only thing keeping us
afloat was our locked gaze,
how will either of us aid in the other's
rescue?

BROKEN

When you gaze back upon
the broken pieces what do you see?
Do you pick them up and rub the
jagged edges till your hands bleed like mine?
And when the pain retreats does it leave
a happy memory that wraps itself
around you while you pray it won't let go?
If anything was wasted it was
the times spent angry and cold
If anything was missing it was the
answers unfound in the fog
Know that I didn't want to leave you
standing there alone
but had to leave the part of me in you
that I could no longer save
so I could save the part of you in me
that will always be in my heart
the part that understands everything
the part that is only love

IV.

LOVE'S REVELATIONS

APRIL'S BREATH

Gazing at the ocean from the top of Malibu Canyon
too hazy to see Catalina but too splendid to take in less
than the deepest breath
my lungs filled up with greater wonder than was there
yesterday
how I found you once upon a time
how I lost you then found you again
how despite the miles between us
my breath can meet your breath as though one breath

A chorus of seagulls serenades me while
I stand peacefully fragmented yet remarkably whole
the sun caresses the crown of my head
like a christening
and the ocean gazes back at me
tenderly whispering
breathe

WHISPERS ON A WINTER'S DAY FAR AWAY

Above our heads sheets of cobalt blue
blessed this day while goodbyes to Grandpa
made their way through tears
Later but what seemed quickly, night fell
and sprinkled snowflakes and smeared
cold wind on my cheeks
After everyone was gone I could see
the ghosts moving about
could see their warm smiles icy now
could feel their tight hugs steely now
could hear their whispers
I wanted to ask Mother and Dad
if they felt them, too
so I would know if it was just me
but instead went to my room and said
two prayers
one for Grandpa
and another that some lucky star
behind the snow clouds would watch over you
while you sleep

STAY CLOSE BY

Stay close by and
not just in my dreams
I long to see how the years have
sculpted your face and how the love
of those who have loved you
has brought warmth to the palm of your hand
I was once among them

BALLET

For a moment I was that whole person
the one dancing on the line between
the dark and the light
satisfied by my oneness with everything
giddy and graceful and spinning delicately alone
For a moment I imagined you there
felt both your hands resting lightly on my waist
paused to find my ballerina's safe haven
        in your eyes
And like every time since the first time
I looked into them your eyes saved me
For a moment I wasn't frightened by the things
I couldn't control
You lifted me high in the air and
I could see everything that mattered
Not afraid to soar
only afraid to look down
and see which side of the rest of my life
you were standing on

SEASONS

The leaves are turning colors and a cool mist of rain
touched the back of my hand today
I thought of mists of rain with you long ago
cool and rich with the mystery and healing
a cool mist of rain brings with it
>*Back home I turned on a movie and in the movie*
>*there was an aerial shot of hillsides covered in white powder*
>*and a black sedan's tire tracks carving their way*
>*through the snow*

kind of like snowfalls with you long ago
powdery and fresh with the silence and wonder
new fallen snow brings with it
   In the movie winter gave way to spring
I remembered springs we'd shared
gentle and pure and wrapped in the frivolity of love
that spring brings with it
>*and when the movie ended*
>*I thought my thoughts of you would, too*
>*but*

I heard the buried whispers of summer that travel
down the paths it forges for itself
and I smelled the sweet breezes it launches
into the air
a warm and fragrant scent that summer brings with it
>   *and I don't know if I wondered*
>   *or*
>   *if I hoped*

when summer comes back this way again
will the breezes that find their way
to my cheek
bring one that brushed against yours?

LOVE SOMEWHAT LATER

I cannot offer you a twenty-seven
or thirty-seven
or even *slightly-over-forty-year-old body*
only one shaped by a life that's lived
beyond those years
one that wants to call your embrace
its home
one that craves the comfort
of your touch
one that trembles at the thought
of your lips on my skin as they
travel with a road map all their own
I cannot resemble the picture of a
girl in the dreams of a teenage boy
but when the man in you
penetrates the poet in me
I hope you find perfection
in this woman's imperfect frame

WHILE YOU SLEPT

While you slept a breeze floated
up from the prickly pear cactus and
through the window and touched me
gently the way you touch me
It brought back moments from the past
when I pondered if there was someone
out there for me
The breeze caressed me and
warmed me
smiled at me
then left me
and when it was gone all that remained
was closure

V.

LONELINESS

A BOX UNDER THE STAIRS

Driving through Calabasas
there was a balminess rare for this time of year
For a moment I was back in St. Thomas
when life was simpler and peace of mind could be found
in a sun-soaked beach towel wrapped
around my shoulders
If I told you all I require is a place in your heart
and in your brain would you know my
greater need was that
you require something of me?
And if I could know the tiny space where
the outside of your eye meets your temple
would the heaviness in this air be lifted?
Worlds away in a box under the stairs,
is my music of pretty poems
and if my tears fall too heavy to see them
I will follow their sound
I will dance this dance for two before
the mirror until
your reflection appears next to mine

WHERE I CROUCH NOT MOVING

It's black there and silent
beyond silent like no air waves for
sound to travel on in order to be sound
no meditation required
no hypnotic regression to the womb to
address or impress
It's cold there
beyond cold like frozen to death but not dead
I know it well—loneliness
I'm its prey and now with my neck in its jaws
drags me screaming back to its cave
drops me where I crouch not moving
head down
eyes shut
holding my breath so the rats won't detect
my breathing
I pray they come quickly

TRIPLE DIGITS

One hundred three degrees in Los Angeles
walking out of Maria's
I heard Frank Sinatra through the restaurant speakers singing
something about the summer wind
I wondered if he ever felt a summer wind like this one
He had a voice that sounded like
he had felt and seen everything
Today's was only a slight summer wind
but a wind all the same
a blazing breeze strong enough to make my hair and
clothes move with it
a searing heat that sent me hiding further into the memory of
the song
further to wherever the melody would take me
> *I heard a preacher say "forward is the only gear God has"*
> *but it seems there's nowhere to go anymore*
and no ground I've covered can be traveled in reverse
no going back even if the answers
lost through a hole in my pocket are better
the second time around

The fire on my cheeks made me squint behind my sunglasses
to see
I was completely alone on the street
I blamed it on the heat that no one was around
but I couldn't help wondering from this point forward
if my only companion would be no more than
a song

LAYOVERS AND DIVORCES

I woke up and found them all over the walls
the certificates from dance recitals
the award for public speaking
the high school diploma
Shifting my weight to the left and lying on my side now
more awards on a shelf to the right of the dresser
entered my view
first place soccer champions
first place cheerleader competition
all strategically placed
and from my vantage point, without a trace of dust

In this friend's spare room, the melancholia in
my stomach met my own children's childhoods
their hard work and accomplishments,
the first places and the times I told them it was
okay to come in second
and I watched the oozing bile seep slowly out
from behind each wooden plaque and tarnished trophy,
embedded in the viscous mass the unpaired eyeballs
there only to judge me,
the serene powder blue walls grieving
for the life I'd had building rooms such as this

Despite my paralysis my fingertips
felt the edges of cardboard boxes at home
in my garage filled with ceramic flowers made in
kindergarten and accolades and *great jobs!*
not hanging on the walls of the home I failed
to keep together
yet holding memories no less permanent
than the ones in this unfamiliar space

Slow motion lifted me off the bed
and I replaced the turquoise quilt as perfectly
as I'd found it, trusting the remnant of my tears
left on the pillow would
dry before anyone would notice,
then with my thoughts began my descent down
the stairs
hoping the only one my friend would detect
was that I had a plane to catch

HAVEN'T MET YOU

I never noticed how the pink and orange
sun-kissed clouds float at sunset
in a way that's meant only for us
or how the caress of
your hand on my cheek
causes my heart to race
like the beating of soft butterfly wings
I never knew about
the magic you make me believe in
the part of my story untold
the dance of my soul to
the rhythm of yours
because
we have not yet
met

HIDING

Needs are mysterious things
human though they may be
We duck and dance and hide behind them
trying on disguises to find the best fit
grabbing at whatever we can find
to cover up our souls
so with any luck the person out of reach
won't see
won't know
won't stumble upon the
truth in the dark where we
dream of them

VI.

INTROSPECTION

LITTLE DRUMMER GIRL

Not all her gifts were pretty
Some were wrapped in paper bags
with crooked bows and stained ribbon
Some came in boxes of confusion
with the sentiment scratched out a few times
Some were ruined with muddy explanations
while she searched for the right thing to say
There are those who would tell her
    thank you, you shouldn't have
and those who would say
    how thoughtful, what is it?
and sometimes even she herself wasn't
sure of the contents
But now she knows what matters
is to show up with whatever she has
finally understanding that her greatest gift
is the one she marks *'as is'*

AUGUST 25TH

You left me on this day in 2009
It was an equally spectacular one to this
with a stunning blue sky and the brightest of sunshine
and a slight breeze making it not too hot for a
southern California day in late August
It was no surprise at all that you chose a beautiful day
for your journey
You held my hand for so many years
through so many things
yet in your suffering I held yours for merely four
So brief those years seem to me now
Yet how long they must have
seemed to you
Short or long the time was never wasted on us
And when I held your hand for the
very last time I whispered
Mom, if you can hear me, I'm here
Then just like always you waited for me to leave first before
you would go
And though you were indeed finally ready for us to part
I was not

THE TASTE OF COFFEE

Until now I never accepted how
much food had to do with it
For four years we never ate in front
of her and I made sure anyone who
came to visit her knew the rule, too,
announcing it like a warning sign
hammered above the entrance to a
dark cave that once inside,
turning on a flashlight or lighting a
candle, is strictly prohibited
And when the nurse assistant would
bring Joan, the woman in the bed
next to my mother's—*I assume Joan is
dead now*—her meal tray, I would
insist, as standard procedure, the
curtain be pulled around Joan's bed
so my mother couldn't see her eat

Until now I never realized that
because of me, every meal Joan had
while we were in the room, she was
forced to eat it in isolation, hidden
from our eyes like her existence was

something unacceptable, as though
she were being punished for doing
something wrong
Of course, we could still smell Joan's
food through the curtain and most
likely so did my mother, that was the
part I had no control over

A decade has passed since my mother
died, but that food was
taken from her and the tube in her
abdomen was supposed to be a
substitute for it—*Can we just put some
turkey gravy on her lips? my dad and I
asked the doctor one Thanksgiving, not
enough for her to swallow? No, was the
answer, because she might try to and could
choke trying*—I could never accept
until now
or the shame that came with knowing
her suffering caused me pain
and my fear that the shame might
consume me
or the moments, but fewer of them
now, I try to imagine—*a pointless
exercise unworthy of honoring my mother*—
being forbidden from eating anything
the rest of my unknown number of
days,

the daily ritual of my morning coffee
taken from me,
making sure just the right amount of
creamer is poured into the cup first
the never again knowing the taste of
it on my tongue
the never again
the never again
Of this I couldn't write before now

AN ODE TO WRITER'S BLOCK

Words like building blocks heaped in piles
in front of me and behind me
to my left and to my right
No I was not buried yet only frozen
empty
cold
Like lost friends they scattered out of reach before me
Like lost loves they beckoned to be found
to be remembered
to be touched again
from under the rubble I heard
> *Save us, we beg you*
> *Start from anywhere you can*
> *We have no life but for you*
> *You have no life but for us*

A hand with steel fingers gripped my ankle
but left me one leg free to stand
to dream
to begin again
Knowing it was to me the words would
look for salvation
It was from me they would
wait for breath
Knowing or else all of us would
die slowly here together

DISCOVERIES AT THE PARK

You turned four last week and today at the park
I watched you try things that barely a year ago
terrified you down to the tips of your tiny toes
But suddenly today there was no slide too steep
no platform too high
no tunnel too dark and no bright orange spiral
ladder left unconquered by you
Today I saw the flicker of that special something
I pray will sustain you throughout all your days and
I held back my tears until you were perched high
at the top of the sliding board, fearful you would reach
the bottom before I had time to wipe them away
But at the end of your ride you were off to the next
adventure, hardly noticing I was there,
as I knew that someday, just like today,
was the way it's meant to be
And that someday, just like today,
you'd need me miraculously less
than what will feel like only yesterday

OF THIS I AM CERTAIN

I'm pretty sure
it's okay to take my hand and go dancing
for life is beautiful but oh so short and the
love I have for you has much to say
So take my hand for a little while
and let's go dancing, my love
because I'm pretty sure
somewhere deep in my heart
that it will be midnight soon

VII.

AMERICA

AMERICA'S CHILD

O beautiful, for spacious skies
How have we let our children die?
When did the seeds of hatred blossom so grand
in this garden of ashes and smoke?
With this same cement did we pave the streets
of our cities and lay the path to churches where
our mothers will cry?
Did we lie asleep while the
Dark
Soul
Walked
From sea to shining sea?
On what foul milk has it nursed?
In the heart of its hungry, its poor,
Its dark and light of skin, its lost and its
most fortunate of spirit
Our America grieves

Oh, say can you see what we
have bred?
When the empty hearted traveler takes
shelter in our midst, in his eyes do we
not see ourselves?
Have we not heard its feasting 'round our hearth?
Where have we gone?
What is this teacher who has poisoned
our wisdom so and left us to crawl with limbs
so weak that with the fiery dust freedom
sifts shamefully from our grasp?
When among the silent ruins of our ages
we weep and through our tears awaken
brother to brother to
the bombs bursting in air,
where is our flag?

FOR TRAYVON

Tonight a beautiful dark skinned boy is
in America's dreams as she sleeps
holding out his hand
beckoning her to walk with him to a
place where they can
look each other in the eye
face to face
heart to heart
race to race
while he waits patiently
silently
steadfastly
for his America to speak
and earn her right to call herself
his home

BALLOT

For the hope that suffocates in pain
For the anger seeking a voice
For the youth who were taught that
the bully never wins
America must stand and face the mirror
Some will look through tears at their
clenched jaw and struggle to understand
Some will find the color of the grass in their
own yard can never thrive when it's valued
over the color of their neighbor's skin
Some will see the conscience they traded
for the sake of change and quickly turn away
but none will find good
for now we must go out and rescue it
Good is bound and gagged and
held captive somewhere beneath the
concrete that paves Pennsylvania Avenue
And good will need the strength of
each of us to return it safely home

About the Author

Wanda Penalver Bevan was born in Ithaca, New York. As early as elementary school, she was always involved in activities that had a focus on writing; from winning the "Very Best Writing" award for penmanship in the first grade, to editor of the school newspaper in the 12th grade. In between, she recalls being asked by her ninth-grade teacher to write a stage adaptation of O. Henry's 1905 short story, *"The Gift of the Magi"*, which became the school play that year.

When Wanda received her bachelor's degree from Northwestern University, many were surprised that she hadn't studied at the university's Medill School of Journalism. However, after high school, she had decided her interest in writing was second to her passion for theatre, which ultimately became her major.

Following college, Wanda moved to Los Angeles, where she had a mildly successful career in acting for stage and TV. She's also worked as a legal assistant, event specialist, and hotel industry professional. Throughout these career changes, Wanda continued to write.

In addition to two screenplays, she's the songwriter of *Little Girl*, a tribute to the youngest victim of the 2011 Tucson shooting, and her poem *America's Child* is on display at the Oklahoma City National Memorial honoring those who lost their lives in the Murrah Federal Building bombing in 1995. In 2016, she published her first novel, *Their Souls Met in Wishton*.

Wanda lives in Phoenix, Arizona, after residing three decades in southern California, whose ocean shores will always have a piece of her heart. She loves to travel, and doesn't fully trust anyone who doesn't like animals. Greater than any gift she's received in life, are her three daughters, and she hopes to become just like them when she grows up.

Acknowledgements

There are many individuals to whom I owe gratitude.

First, to my parents, Marge and Ted, for encouraging me throughout my life and supporting me in whatever I pursued. They are my angels watching over me.

To my family and friends, for believing in me and always standing by me. You make me feel like I "fit in", when having the soul of an artist leaves you perpetually doubtful that you do. Your presence in my life is never taken for granted.

Thank you to my editor Ian Hooper at The Book Reality Experience, whose first response after reading my manuscript was, "I love your poems." That was all the encouragement I needed to believe this collection was worth publishing.

To Russell, thank you for loving me in a way that astounds me.

To my amazing daughters, Amanda, Rosalind and Madison, thank you for reminding me every day that there are miracles to be found in every moment if you simply look for them, and who I love more than any words in a book could ever describe.

Finally, to My Creator, I give thanks for the safety net I cannot see but is always there when I leap.

www.ingramcontent.com/pod-product-compliance
Lightning Source LLC
Chambersburg PA
CBHW021448080526
44588CB00009B/750